Above and Below the Extremes

Finding Stability with Bipolar Disorder

Deepak Singh

 pencil

ISBN 978-93-5667-715-9
© Deepak Singh 2023

Published in India 2023 by Pencil

A brand of
One Point Six Technologies Pvt. Ltd.
Unit no. 26, Ground Floor, Building A1,
Wadala Truck Terminal Road,
Near Post Office, Antop Hill, Mumbai - 400037
E connect@thepencilapp.com
W www.thepencilapp.com

DISCLAIMER: *The opinions expressed in this book are those of the authors and do not purport to reflect the views of the Publisher.*

Author biography

Hello! Happy to meet you, I'm Deepak Singh. I work as a research analyst and am passionate about writing books and doing research on the planet Earth, space, and the art of living. I most likely have high analytical and critical thinking abilities that enable me to assess data, spot trends, and reach conclusions in my capacity as a research analyst. As part of my job, I might perform primary and secondary research, analyze available data, and provide findings to guide individual, corporate, or organizational decision-making. I adore writing and researching as interests in space and Earth in my free time. You can tell that I have an open mind and am interested in learning about the world around me.

CONTENTS

Introduction

Bipolar Disorder is a complex and difficult disorder that affects millions of people around the world. It is a mental health condition characterized by mania, hypomania, and depression. These episodes can be intense and disruptive, affecting all aspects of a person's life, from work and relationships to physical and emotional health.

Recovery from Bipolar Disorder can be a long and arduous road, but it is achievable. It is possible to attain stability and live a full life with the correct tools, resources, and support. This book, "Above and Below the Extremes: Finding Stability with Bipolar Disorder," is intended to help those who have Bipolar Disorder, their loved ones, and mental health professionals navigate this journey.

We will explore the essentials of Bipolar Disorder, including its forms, symptoms, and causes, in this book. We will also look into the various treatment choices, such as medication management, psychotherapy, and lifestyle changes. We'll look at coping tactics for hypomania, mania, and depression, as well as anxiety and panic attacks. We will also talk about how to build resilience and good relationships, how to deal with stigma and prejudice, and how to advocate for yourself and others.

This book is not intended to replace medical advice or treatment, but rather to encourage those living with Bipolar Disorder to take control of their recovery journey. We hope that this book will provide readers with useful ideas and practical skills to help them establish stability, build resilience, and live a full life beyond the highs and lows of Bipolar Disorder.

Note: The term "drugs" in this book refers to medicines recommended by a Doctor to treat bipolar disorder.

Chapter 1 Bipolar Disorder An Overview

What exactly is Bipolar Disorder?

Manic-depressive disease, also known as bipolar disorder, is a mental health condition characterized by significant variations in mood, energy, activity levels, and behavior. Bipolar disorder patients may have episodes of mania or hypomania, periods of depression, or a combination of the two. These episodes can vary in strength and frequency, and they can severely disrupt a person's life.

Bipolar disorder affects about 2.6% of the US population, with an average onset age of around 25 years. It affects men and women equally and is present in all racial and ethnic groupings. While the specific origin of bipolar disease is unknown, a combination of genetic, environmental, and neurological factors is thought to be involved.

Bipolar disorder is classified into various categories, each with its unique set of symptoms and patterns. Bipolar I disorder is the most severe form of the condition, with manic episodes lasting at least a week or necessitating hospitalization. Depressive episodes may occur, however, they are not necessary for diagnosis. Bipolar II disorder is characterized by hypomanic episodes that are less severe than manic episodes but are nevertheless disruptive to a person's life. Bipolar II condition includes major depression episodes.

Cyclothymic disorder is a subtype of bipolar disorder characterized by bouts of hypomania and mild depression. These episodes may not be severe enough to qualify as a full manic or depressive episode, yet they can nevertheless have a substantial impact on an individual's life. Unspecified bipolar disorder and bipolar disorder not otherwise specified are two further kinds of bipolar disorder.

Manic episodes are the hallmark of bipolar disorder, and they are distinguished by an elevated or irritated mood, heightened energy, racing thoughts, and risky behavior. Individuals experiencing a manic episode may engage in dangerous behaviors such as spending sprees, substance addiction, or sexual promiscuity. They may also have hallucinations or delusions.

Hypomanic episodes are comparable to manic episodes, but they are less intense and do not have a substantial impact on a person's life. Individuals may be more productive and social than usual during a hypomanic episode, but they may also engage in impulsive or dangerous behavior.

Depressive episodes, which are characterized by a gloomy or irritable mood, lack of interest or pleasure in activities, changes in eating and sleep habits, exhaustion, and feelings of worthlessness or guilt, are also common in bipolar illness. During a depressed episode, suicidal thoughts or behaviors may also be present.

Bipolar disorder is normally treated with a mix of medication and psychotherapy. Lithium and valproic acid are common mood stabilizers used to assist regulate mood and avoid manic or depressed episodes. Antidepressants can be used to treat depressive episodes, but they should be used with caution because they might cause manic or hypomanic episodes in some people.

Individuals with bipolar disorder can benefit from psychotherapy, such as cognitive-behavioral therapy or interpersonal therapy, to help them control their symptoms, cope with stress, and enhance their relationships. In severe or treatment-resistant cases of bipolar illness, electroconvulsive therapy (ECT) may be prescribed.

Living with bipolar disorder can be difficult, but with adequate treatment and support, people with the diagnosis can live full and productive lives. Individuals suffering from bipolar disorder should have a strong support network of family, friends, and mental health specialists, as well as be actively involved in their own treatment and rehabilitation.

To summarise, bipolar disorder is a complex and difficult mental health illness that can significantly affect an individual's life. Individuals with bipolar disorder, however, can learn to manage their symptoms and have full and productive lives with proper diagnosis, medication, and support. Individuals suffering from bipolar disorder should seek help from mental health specialists, actively participate in their therapy, and develop a strong support network. We can help improve the lives of persons afflicted by bipolar disorder by increasing awareness and reducing stigma.

Bipolar Disorder Types

Bipolar disorder is distinguished by episodes of mania or hypomania, depression, or a combination of the two. There are various forms of bipolar disorder, each with its own set of symptoms and treatment choices.

This chapter will look at the many types of bipolar disorder and its characteristics: Bipolar I Disorder: The most severe form of bipolar disorder is bipolar I disorder. Bipolar I patients have manic episodes that last at least seven days, and they frequently require hospitalization to control their symptoms. Individuals with bipolar I disorder may experience an exaggerated feeling of self-esteem or grandiosity, a decreased need for sleep, racing thoughts, and impulsive behavior during manic episodes. They may also engage in unsafe behaviors such as reckless driving or excessive spending. People with bipolar I disorder may also have depressive episodes that last at least two weeks.

- **Bipolar II Disorder:**Although bipolar II condition is milder than bipolar I disorder, it can nevertheless have a substantial influence on a person's life. Hypomanic episodes are less intense than manic episodes in people with bipolar II illness. Hypomanic episodes last at least four days and are distinguished by heightened activity, a reduced need for sleep, and racing thoughts. In contrast to manic episodes, hypomanic episodes have no significant impact on a person's life.

People with bipolar II disorder also have depression episodes that last at least two weeks.

- **Cyclothymic Disorder:**Cyclothymic disorder is a milder form of bipolar illness characterized by frequent phases of hypomania and depression that do not match the criteria for bipolar I or bipolar II disorder. The cyclothymic disorder causes frequent mood fluctuations that last at least two years in adults and one year in children and adolescents. These mood swings can be quite upsetting and affect a person's ability to operate properly.

- **Other Bipolar and Related Disorders, Specified and Unspecified:**This category comprises bipolar disorders that do not fall into any of the other categories. This comprises unspecified bipolar disorder (NOS) and other specified bipolar and associated disorders (OSBRD). People with bipolar NOS have bipolar disorder symptoms that do not fulfill the criteria for any other kind of bipolar disorder. OSBRD encompasses bipolar disorders that do not fall into any of the other categories, such as rapid cycling bipolar disorder, which is defined by four or more episodes of mania, hypomania, or depression in a year.

Diagnosis and Symptoms

The disorder is distinguished by extreme highs, known as manic or hypomanic episodes, and extreme lows, known as depressed episodes. These episodes can last days, weeks, or even months and are severe enough to interfere with a person's everyday life.

Bipolar Disorder Diagnosis:

Bipolar illness is a complex mental health issue that necessitates an in-depth assessment and diagnosis by a mental health specialist. A thorough physical and psychological examination, as well as a study of the patient's medical and family history, are often used to make a diagnosis.

The diagnostic procedure may comprise the following steps:

- **Clinical interview:**During the clinical interview, the mental health professional may inquire about the patient's symptoms, family history, and medical history. They may also inquire about earlier experiences of mania or depression, as well as how the patient dealt with them.

- **Mood charting:**Mood charting entails keeping a daily record of mood fluctuations, including highs and lows, as well as any triggers that may have played a role in them.

- **Psychological evaluation:**A battery of tests to assess cognitive function, personality traits, and emotional states may be included in a psychological evaluation.

- **Medical tests:**Blood tests, imaging tests, and other medical exams may be performed to rule out any underlying medical disorders that may be contributing to the patient's symptoms.

Bipolar Disorder Symptoms:

Bipolar disorder symptoms can vary based on the type of episode and the severity of the condition. Manic or hypomanic episodes and depressive episodes are the two basic forms of episodes.

Episodes of mania or hypomania:

A person may experience the following symptoms during a manic or hypomanic episode:

- **Elevated mood:**Extremely pleasant or euphoric feelings.

- **Increased energy levels:**restlessness, inability to sit motionless, and a high level of activity.

- **Impulsive behaviors:**Engaging in impulsive behaviors such as shopping sprees, sexual promiscuity, or risky driving.

- **Reduced sleep:**Reduced sleep requirement: Feeling energized despite not sleeping for long periods of time.

- **Racing thoughts:**Having disorganized, fast thoughts that are difficult to regulate.

- **Grandiosity:**Grandiosity is defined as a heightened sense of self-importance, inflated beliefs in one's talents, and a sense of invincibility.

- **Irritability:**The ability to become easily annoyed or irritable.

Episodes of depression:

A person may have the following symptoms during a depressed episode:

- **Sadness or hopelessness:**Feeling depressed or blue, with a sensation that things will never get better.

- **Loss of interest:**Loss of interest refers to a loss of interest in formerly enjoyable activities such as hobbies or socializing.

- **Appetite and sleep changes:**Having an increased or decreased appetite, or sleeping too much or too little.

- **Fatigue:**Exhaustion or a lack of energy.

- **Difficulty concentrating:**Having difficulty focusing on tasks or retaining information.

- **Guilt or worthlessness:**A sense of guilt, worthlessness, or shame.

- **Suicidal ideation:**Having suicidal thoughts or attempting suicide.

It is critical to remember that bipolar disease is a highly treatable condition and that with proper treatment, many people with bipolar disorder can live full and productive lives. Consult a mental health professional if you or a loved one are experiencing signs of bipolar illness.

Factors of Risk and Causes

Although the causes of bipolar illness are not fully known, experts have found some risk factors for the condition.

- **Genetics:**Genetics is a significant risk factor for bipolar disorder. According to research, bipolar disorder runs in families, and persons who have a close relative with the disorder are more likely to have it themselves. However, bipolar disorder is not caused only by genetics, and many people with a family history of the disorder never get it.

- **Structure and function of the brain:**Differences in brain structure and function have also been linked to the development of bipolar disorder. People suffering from bipolar disorder may exhibit abnormalities in the size and activity of specific brain regions, such as the prefrontal cortex and the amygdala.

- **Environmental considerations:**While genetics and brain function are important variables in the development of bipolar disease, environmental factors are equally important. Some people can develop bipolar disorder as a result of trauma, abuse, or stressful life circumstances. Substance misuse, such as alcohol and drug use, can also raise the likelihood of having bipolar illness.

- **Medical problems:**Certain medical issues can also raise the likelihood of developing bipolar disorder. People with thyroid issues, multiple sclerosis, and Parkinson's disease, for example, may be predisposed to bipolar disorder. Furthermore, certain drugs, such as antidepressants and steroids, might cause manic or hypomanic episodes in some people.

- **Childhood memories:**Childhood events, according to research, can also have a role in the development of bipolar disorder. Children who are abused or neglected, or who grow up in unstable situations, are at a higher risk of developing the illness later in life.

To summarise, bipolar disorder is a complicated syndrome influenced by a mix of hereditary, environmental, and neurological variables. While the specific causes of bipolar illness are unknown, identifying and addressing risk factors early on can help persons with the condition manage their symptoms and improve their outcomes.

To summarise, bipolar disorder is a complicated syndrome influenced by a mix of hereditary, environmental, and neurological variables. While the specific causes of bipolar illness are unknown, identifying and addressing risk factors early on can help persons with the condition manage their symptoms and improve their outcomes.

Chapter 2 Medications for Bipolar Disorder

Common medications used for Bipolar Disorder

Medications are an important aspect of bipolar disorder treatment. They aid in the management of symptoms, the stabilization of mood, and the prevention of relapses. We will address the most commonly used drugs for bipolar disorder in this response.

- **Mood Stabilisers:**The most commonly used drugs for bipolar disorder are mood stabilizers. They aid in the prevention of mood fluctuations and the danger of relapse. Among the most widely used mood stabilizers are:

- **Lithium:**One of the oldest mood stabilizers, lithium is still frequently used today. It has the potential to be very beneficial in preventing manic episodes and lowering the risk of suicide. However, because it has a narrow therapeutic range, blood levels must be continuously managed to avoid toxicity.

- **Valproic Acid (Depakote):**Another regularly used mood stabilizer is valproic acid. It has the potential to be beneficial in treating both manic and depressive episodes. However, it can cause weight gain and hair loss as adverse effects.

- **Carbamazepine (Tegretol):**Carbamazepine is another mood stabilizer that can help in bipolar disorder treatment. It can assist to prevent manic episodes and lower the likelihood of relapse. However, it may cause dizziness and nausea in some people.

- **Antipsychotics:**Antipsychotics are also routinely used to treat bipolar disorder, particularly during manic periods. They can assist to alleviate symptoms like delusions, hallucinations, and irritation. Among the most often used antipsychotics are:

- **Olanzapine:**Olanzapine is an atypical antipsychotic that has been shown to be useful in the treatment of manic episodes. However, it may cause weight gain and a rise in the risk of diabetes.

- **Quetiapine:**Quetiapine (Seroquel) is another atypical antipsychotic that can help with both manic and depressive episodes. It can also aid with anxiety and sleep. However, it may cause sleepiness and dizziness in certain people.

- **Aripiprazole:**Aripiprazole (Abilify) is a newer atypical antipsychotic that can be used to treat both manic and depressive episodes. It is less likely to cause weight gain and metabolic side effects than other antipsychotics.

- **Antidepressants:**Antidepressants are sometimes used to treat bipolar disorder's depression periods. They can, however, raise the risk of manic episodes and should be used with caution. Among the most widely used antidepressants arc:

- **Selective Serotonin Reuptake Inhibitors:**Selective Serotonin Reuptake Inhibitors (SSRIs): SSRIs are antidepressants that can be beneficial in the treatment of depressive episodes. They can, however, raise the risk of manic episodes and should be used with caution.

- **Bupropion:**Bupropion (Wellbutrin): Bupropion is an antidepressant that can be beneficial in treating bipolar disorder depressive episodes. However, it may cause anxiety and insomnia in certain people.

It is critical to remember that bipolar disorder drugs should always be taken under the supervision of a healthcare expert. They can assist in determining the appropriate prescription and dose for each individual, as well as monitoring for adverse effects and drug interactions.

Note: The term "drugs" refers to medicines recommended by a Doctor to treat bipolar disorder.

How to manage medication effectively:

Bipolar disorder is a chronic mental health illness characterized by significant mood fluctuations ranging from mania (or hypomania) to depression (or depression). Medication is an important aspect of managing bipolar disease since it can help stabilize mood, lessen symptoms, and prevent relapses.

Here are some pointers for efficiently managing bipolar illness medication:

- **Follow your doctor's advice:**It is critical that you take your prescription exactly as directed by your doctor. Do not alter or discontinue your medicine without first visiting your doctor.

- **Use a pill organizer:**A pill organizer can assist you in keeping track of your meds and ensuring that you take them on time. To help you remember to take your prescription, set a reminder on your phone or use a calendar.

- **Maintain a medication log:**Keep a note of your medication, including the medication's name, dosage, and any side effects you experience. At each appointment, share this information with your doctor so that they can change your treatment plan as needed.

- **Do not skip doses:**Skipping a medicine dose can interrupt your treatment plan and raise your chance of relapse. If you forget to take your medication, take it as soon as you recall or get advice from your doctor.

- **Be mindful of potential side effects:**Some drugs used to treat bipolar disorder can have negative side effects. Weight gain, sleepiness, tremors, and blurred vision are some of the symptoms. If you have side effects, consult your doctor, who may alter your medication or recommend a new drug.

- **Keep your doctor informed:**If you notice any changes in your mood, sleeping patterns, or other symptoms, notify your doctor right away. To properly manage your symptoms, they may need to change your prescription or treatment strategy.

- **Avoid alcohol and drugs:**These substances can interfere with your medicine and increase your chances of relapse. It is critical to avoid alcohol and drugs when on bipolar disorder medication.

In summary, effectively managing medication for bipolar disorder entails following your doctor's instructions, using a pill organizer, maintaining a medication diary, not skipping doses, being mindful of adverse effects, informing your doctor, and abstaining from alcohol and drugs. It is possible to manage bipolar disease efficiently and enhance your quality of life with the correct treatment plan and support.

Chapter 3 Psychotherapy for Bipolar Disorder

Types of psychotherapy used for Bipolar Disorder

It is a complex disorder that necessitates a multifaceted treatment strategy that includes medication, counseling, and lifestyle adjustments.

Psychotherapy, commonly known as talk therapy, is a type of treatment that assists persons suffering from bipolar disorder in recognizing and managing their symptoms. There are various types of psychotherapy available to treat bipolar disorder, each with its own approach and benefits.

Here are some of the most popular types of bipolar disorder psychotherapy:

- **Cognitive-behavioral therapy (CBT):**CBT is a type of therapy that assists patients suffering from bipolar disorder in identifying and changing problematic thought patterns and behaviors. It is a systematic, brief therapy that focuses on specific problems and objectives. People who participate in CBT learn skills to assist them to manage their symptoms, such as developing coping techniques for stressors and recognizing early warning signals of a mood episode.

- **Interpersonal and social rhythm therapy (IPSRT):**IPSRT is a type of therapy that focuses on establishing and maintaining daily routines and social rhythms, such as sleep, eating, and exercise, in order to assist control of mood disorders. This therapy also focuses on enhancing interpersonal relationships and communication skills, both of which can suffer during mood swings.

- **FFT (family-focused therapy):**FFT is a sort of therapy in which family members participate in the treatment process. It attempts to increase family communication and problem-solving abilities, reduce stress, and strengthen family relationships. Because teenagers and young adults with bipolar disorder frequently rely on their families for support, FFT can be especially beneficial.

- **Psychoeducation:**Psychoeducation is a sort of therapy that assists persons with bipolar disorder in understanding their condition and learning how to manage it. It is available in individual or group settings and includes topics such as bipolar disease biology, medication administration, and coping skills.

- **Psychodynamic therapy:**Psychodynamic therapy is a type of therapy that focuses on identifying and resolving underlying emotional problems that may contribute to the symptoms of bipolar illness. Its goal is to assist people to acquire insight into their ideas, feelings, and behaviors so that they can make positive changes in their life.

- **Mindfulness:**Mindfulness-based therapy is a style of therapy that focuses on present-moment mindfulness and acceptance of thoughts and feelings. It can assist persons with bipolar disorder in reducing stress, improving mood, and developing coping mechanisms for symptom management.

Overall, the type of psychotherapy used to treat bipolar disorder may be determined by a number of factors, including the individual's preferences, the severity of their symptoms, and the level of support they receive from family and friends. Working with a mental health specialist to determine the best effective treatment strategy for your specific requirements is critical.

Benefits of psychotherapy

These mood fluctuations can have a substantial influence on an individual's life and relationships, making it critical to successfully manage the disease. Psychotherapy is one of the most successful therapies for bipolar disorder, offering a variety of benefits that can help individuals manage their symptoms and improve their quality of life.

Here are some of the advantages of bipolar disorder psychotherapy:

Psychotherapy can help people understand and manage their symptoms: Psychotherapy can assist people with bipolar disorder understand their symptoms and how they affect their life. They can learn to recognize triggers, develop coping techniques, and control their symptoms more successfully through therapy.

Reduces the chance of relapse: People who have bipolar disorder are at a significant risk of relapse, which can be triggered by stress, lifestyle changes, or other circumstances. Psychotherapy can help lower the likelihood of relapse by giving individuals with the skills and resources they need to effectively manage their symptoms.

Improves medication adherence: Psychotherapy can assist patients with bipolar disorder in understanding the importance of medication adherence and in addressing any problems or challenges they may be experiencing with their drug regimen.

Provides emotional support: Living with bipolar disorder can be difficult, and people may feel alienated, misunderstood, or stigmatized. Psychotherapy can offer emotional support as well as a secure area for people to express their thoughts and feelings without fear of being judged.

Improves communication skills: Bipolar disease can impair communication skills, resulting in misunderstandings and confrontations with loved ones. Individuals can benefit from psychotherapy by improving their communication skills, which can improve their relationships and reduce stress.

Helps with lifestyle adjustments: Psychotherapy can assist patients suffering from bipolar disorder in making lifestyle changes that will benefit their mental health, such as improving sleep habits, lowering stress, and boosting physical activity.

Improves quality of life: Psychotherapy can considerably improve the quality of life for people with bipolar disorder by improving symptom management, lowering the risk of relapse, giving emotional support, and increasing communication skills.

Finally, psychotherapy is an effective treatment for bipolar disease that provides a variety of benefits such as increased symptom management, decreased risk of relapse, emotional support, improved communication skills, and improved quality of life. If you or a loved one has bipolar illness, it is critical to consult with a mental health professional to identify the best appropriate treatment strategy for your specific requirements.

Finding a therapist and making the most of therapy sessions

It can be a difficult condition to manage, and therapy can be an effective treatment option for Bipolar Disorder. Here are some pointers to help you locate a therapist and get the most out of your treatment sessions.

- **Choosing a Therapist:**Request a referral from your primary care physician to a mental health specialist who specializes in Bipolar Disorder.

- **Search online:**Use internet directories or search engines to identify therapists in your region who have worked with Bipolar Disorder.

- **Request suggestions:**Ask friends, relatives, or support groups for therapist referrals who have helped them with their Bipolar Disorder.

- **Examine credentials:**Ensure that the therapist you select is licensed and has expertise working with persons who have Bipolar Disorder.

- **Consider the following:**Check with your insurance company to check if the therapist you're interested in is covered.

Getting the Most Out of Therapy Sessions

- **Be truthful:**Tell your therapist the truth about your symptoms and experiences. This will assist your therapist in creating an effective treatment plan.

- **Set precise goals:**Set precise goals for your treatment sessions in collaboration with your therapist. This will assist you in remaining focused and making progress.

- **Ask your therapist:**Ask your therapist to teach you coping techniques that will help you manage your mood fluctuations.

- **Commitment:**Maintain your commitment by attending therapy sessions on a regular basis and actively engaging in the process.

- **Be receptive to input:**Be open to feedback from your therapist and willing to adjust your treatment plan as needed.

Chapter 4 Lifestyle Changes for Managing Bipolar Disorder

The importance of sleep, exercise, and nutrition

Although there is no cure for bipolar disorder, symptoms can be managed with a combination of medication, treatment, and lifestyle adjustments. Sleep, exercise, and nutrition, in particular, are all essential elements that can influence the duration and severity of bipolar disease.

- **Sleep:**Sleep is vital for optimal mental health, and sleep disruptions can initiate or exacerbate bipolar symptoms. Sleep difficulties, such as insomnia or hypersomnia, are common in people with bipolar disorder. Maintaining a consistent sleep schedule and practicing good sleep hygiene, such as avoiding coffee and electronics before bed, can help improve sleep quality and lessen bipolar illness symptoms.

- **Exercise:**Exercise has been demonstrated to offer numerous benefits for patients with bipolar disorder, including reduced symptoms of despair and anxiety, improved cognitive performance, and improved overall quality of life. Exercise can also help regulate mood and promote sleep, all of which are important variables in bipolar illness management. However, it is critical to begin gradually and collaborate with a healthcare physician to build a safe and effective exercise regimen.

- **Nutrition:**Eating a healthy, balanced diet can also help with bipolar disorder. Certain dietary patterns, such as the Mediterranean diet, have been demonstrated in studies to improve mood and cognitive function in patients with bipolar disorder. Furthermore, certain foods, such as omega-3 fatty acids and vitamin D, have been demonstrated to protect against bipolar disorder. It is critical to collaborate with a healthcare professional or registered dietitian to create a dietary plan that fulfills individual needs while also supporting overall health.

Finally, sleep, exercise, and nutrition are all essential elements that might influence the severity and course of bipolar disease. While these lifestyle modifications are not a replacement for medicine and therapy, incorporating them into a treatment plan can help control symptoms and improve overall quality of life. Working with a healthcare provider to build a comprehensive treatment plan that addresses all components of bipolar illness is critical.

Reducing stress and triggers

These mood fluctuations might be accompanied by high levels of stress and worry, which can induce or exacerbate symptoms. Managing stress and detecting triggers are critical components of bipolar illness treatment. Here are some suggestions for lowering stress and stressors when dealing with bipolar disorder:

- **Stick to a Routine:**A routine can help to reduce stress and provide a sense of stability. Part of this is establishing regular schedules for sleeping, eating, exercising, and other daily responsibilities.

- **Stay Active:**A routine can help to reduce stress and provide a sense of stability. Part of this is establishing regular schedules for sleeping, eating, exercising, and other daily responsibilities.

- **Avoid Triggers:**Determine what causes your mood fluctuations and strive to avoid them. Certain meals, stressful situations, or even specific persons may fall into this category.

- **Learn Relaxation Techniques:**Relaxation techniques such as deep breathing, meditation, and progressive muscle relaxation can all assist to reduce stress and anxiety. These techniques can be used at any time, but they are especially beneficial during times of extreme stress.

- **Get Enough Sleep:**Sleep deprivation can cause mood changes, so it's critical to stick to a regular sleep pattern and get enough rest each night. Sleep for 7-9 hours per night.

- **Self-Care is vital:**Self-care is vital for controlling bipolar disorder. Consuming a good diet, abstaining from alcohol and drugs, and indulging in activities that offer you joy and relaxation are all part of this.

- **Seek Help:**Having a support system is essential for dealing with bipolar disorder. Family, friends, or a mental health professional can all be included. Participating in a support group might also be beneficial.

Overall, stress and trigger management is an important element of controlling the bipolar disorder. Individuals with bipolar disorder can minimize stress and enhance their general well-being by developing a routine, staying active, avoiding triggers, learning relaxation techniques, getting enough sleep, practicing self-care, and seeking assistance. Working with a mental health specialist to establish a thorough treatment plan that suits your specific requirements is critical.

Developing a support system

The disorder can have a substantial impact on a person's daily life, including relationships, jobs, and overall well-being. Creating a strong support system can be critical in controlling bipolar disorder symptoms and enhancing the quality of life for those affected by the condition.

Here are some ideas for creating a bipolar support system:

- **Seek professional help:**Seeking professional help is the first step in creating a support system for bipolar disorder. This may entail consulting with a therapist or psychiatrist, who will diagnose the problem and devise a treatment plan. Medication, therapy, or a mix of the two may be used in treatment.

- **Educate yourself and others:**It is critical that you and others learn about bipolar disorder. This can help you understand the condition better and inform others on how to help. Support groups and educational programs are among the many services accessible online and in the community.

- **Create a network of people who will be there for you:**Building a network of supportive people can be quite beneficial in dealing with bipolar disease. This may include family members, friends, or members of a support group who are familiar with the condition and can provide emotional support when needed. You can also seek help from organizations that specialize in bipolar disorder, such as the National Alliance on Mental Illness (NAMI).

- **Create a self-care routine:**Self-care is an essential component of controlling bipolar disorder. This may include regular exercise, adequate sleep, a good diet, and participation in activities that you enjoy. Creating a self-care practice can assist you in managing stress and improving your overall well-being.

- **Develop a crisis plan:**In the event of a bipolar episode, it is critical to have a crisis plan in place. This may include identifying triggers, developing a treatment plan, and knowing who to contact in an emergency

Finally, building a support system for persons suffering from bipolar illness can be critical in controlling the condition and enhancing the quality of life for those affected. Seeking professional assistance, educating yourself and others, establishing a network of supportive individuals, forming a self-care routine, and making a crisis plan are all critical elements in constructing a solid support system. Individuals with bipolar disease can live productive and meaningful lives with the correct assistance.

Chapter 5 Building Resilience

Coping strategies for managing episodes

Coping with bipolar disorder can be difficult, especially during intense mood swings. There are, however, various coping skills that can assist individuals in managing their symptoms and leading a satisfying life.

Medication Management: Medication management is one of the most significant strategies for managing bipolar disorder. Medications such as mood stabilisers, antidepressants, and antipsychotics can aid in mood regulation and the prevention of episodes. Working with a healthcare expert to identify the proper medication and dose for your specific needs is critical.

Therapy: Therapy can also be beneficial in the treatment of bipolar disorder. Cognitive-behavioral therapy (CBT) and psychotherapy can assist individuals in identifying triggers and developing coping skills for symptom management. Group therapy and support groups can also help to foster a sense of belonging and support.

Adjustments in Lifestyle: Lifestyle adjustments such as regular exercise, a good diet, and appropriate sleep can help regulate emotions and prevent episodes. Avoiding drugs and alcohol, as well as sticking to a regular regimen, can be useful.

Stress Management: Stress management is critical for those with bipolar disorder since it can provoke episodes. Mindfulness, deep breathing, and meditation are all techniques that can help people manage stress and minimize their chances of having an episode.

Support System: Having a support system is critical when dealing with bipolar disorder. Family members, friends, healthcare practitioners, and support groups can all be included. During episodes, it is critical to have people who can provide emotional support as well as help with practical duties.

Self-Care: Self-care is also essential for controlling bipolar disorder. This can include engaging in enjoyable activities such as hobbies or artistic endeavors. Making time for oneself and practicing relaxation techniques might also help.

To summarise, controlling bipolar disorder can be difficult, but with the correct tactics and support, people can live satisfying lives. It is critical to collaborate with a healthcare professional to design a treatment plan that is tailored to each individual.

Identifying warning signs and early intervention

These mood fluctuations can be strong enough to impair daily living and result in a variety of undesirable outcomes, such as interpersonal issues, job loss, and substance abuse.

Identifying warning signals and responding early in the course of bipolar disorder is critical for preventing the condition from worsening and increasing the likelihood of successful treatment. Here are some bipolar disorder warning signals and early intervention strategies:

- **Pay attention to mood fluctuations:**People with bipolar disorder frequently experience mood shifts that are out of proportion to the environment or triggers. It is critical to seek help from a mental health expert if you observe sudden changes in mood or behavior.

- **Monitor sleep patterns:**Changes in sleep patterns are frequently an early warning indication of a bipolar episode. If you realize that you are sleeping excessively or insufficiently, it is necessary to see a mental health expert.

- **Maintain an eye on your energy levels:**Bipolar disorder can produce dramatic swings in your energy levels. Individuals may report greater activity, restlessness, and a decreased need for sleep during manic or hypomanic episodes. They may feel fatigued and have difficulties getting out of bed during depressive periods. Monitoring your energy levels can assist you in identifying warning signs and intervening early.

- **Seek help:**Having a supportive network of family and friends might help with bipolar disease management. When you are suffering symptoms or need someone to talk to, reach out to loved ones.

- **Take medication as prescribed:**Medication can be an effective treatment for bipolar disorder, but it only works if taken exactly as prescribed. It is critical to consult with a mental health specialist to determine the best medicine and dose for your symptoms.

- **Attend therapy:**Therapy can help with bipolar disorder treatment by teaching coping strategies, stress management techniques, and a secure space to communicate about your experiences.

Finally, recognizing warning signals and intervening early in the course of bipolar illness can help prevent the condition from worsening and increase the odds of successful treatment. If you are suffering symptoms or have worries about your mental health, it is critical that you seek help from a mental health expert.

Building resilience and staying positive

Managing bipolar disorder is difficult, and it frequently necessitates a combination of medication, therapy, and lifestyle modifications. Building resilience and remaining optimistic can be helpful in controlling bipolar disorder and enhancing the quality of life.

Here are some suggestions for developing resilience and being optimistic as a bipolar illness patient:

- **Educate yourself on bipolar disorder:**Understanding the nature of the bipolar disorder and how it affects your mood can aid in the identification of triggers and the development of coping techniques. Knowledge can assist you in recognizing early warning signals of a mood episode and intervening to avert a full-blown episode.

- **Maintain a routine:**Having a regular routine can help you stabilize your mood and reduce your chances of having a mood episode. Try to get up and go to bed at the same time every day, eat meals at consistent times, and plan activities and exercise into your day.

- **Self-care:**Taking care of yourself, both physically and mentally, is critical for managing bipolar disease. Maintain healthy behaviors such as eating a balanced diet, getting regular exercise, getting enough sleep, and abstaining from drugs and alcohol. Participate in activities that give you joy and fulfillment.

- **Seek help:**Bipolar disorder can be isolating, but it's critical to remember that you're not alone. Seek emotional assistance from family, friends, and support groups. Consider attending a bipolar disorder support group to connect with individuals who understand what you're going through.

- **Learn coping skills:**Coping skills can assist you in managing stress and preventing mood swings. Deep breathing, meditation, writing, and artistic expression are all examples of coping methods. Discuss with your therapist or mental health practitioner which coping skills could be most beneficial to you.

- **Set and achieve realistic goals:**Setting and attaining realistic goals can aid in the development of self-esteem and a sense of purpose. Begin modestly and gradually progress to higher goals.

- **Concentrate on the positive:**It's easy to become engrossed in negative thinking, especially during depressive episodes. Concentrate on the positive aspects of your life and practice thankfulness for what you have.

It may take some time to figure out what works best for you when it comes to building resilience and staying positive. Be kind to yourself and enjoy your victories along the way. It is possible to live a fulfilling life with bipolar disease if you have the necessary tools and support.

Chapter 6 Managing Hypomania and Mania

Understanding Hypomanic and manic episodes

Hypomania and manic episodes are two types of mood episodes that bipolar disorder patients frequently experience. Understanding the distinctions between these two episodes can aid in the management of the illness.

Hypomania is a lesser version of mania marked by a euphoric or exhilarated attitude, increased energy, a decreased need for sleep, and enhanced confidence. People suffering from hypomania may be more chatty, creative, and friendly than usual. They may also engage in dangerous sexual behavior or participate in impulsive behaviors such as shopping sprees. Hypomania is less severe than a full-blown manic episode and does not usually affect social or occupational functioning significantly.

Manic episodes, on the other hand, are far more severe and can be life-threatening. They have an unusually elevated or angry mood, a decreased need for sleep, and a lot of activity. People experiencing manic episodes may indulge in grandiose thinking and believe they are invincible or unstoppable. They may also have racing thoughts, speak fast, and move from one issue to the next. Manic episodes can affect social and vocational functioning significantly and may necessitate hospitalization.

Bipolar disorder is connected with both hypomanic and manic episodes, which can be difficult to treat. Medication, such as mood stabilisers and antipsychotics, as well as counseling and lifestyle adjustments, are commonly used in treatment. Individuals suffering from bipolar disorder may benefit from establishing coping methods to control their symptoms, such as avoiding triggers and practicing relaxation techniques.

Finally, recognizing hypomanic and manic episodes in bipolar illness is critical for disease management. Hypomania is a less severe form of mania that usually does not cause considerable damage. Manic episodes, on the other hand, are more severe and can be harmful, impairing social and vocational functioning significantly. Medication, therapy, and lifestyle modifications are common treatments, and establishing coping mechanisms can help control symptoms. If you or a loved one is suffering signs of bipolar disorder, it is critical that you seek professional care.

Identifying Triggers and early warning signs

Bipolar disorder, commonly known as manic-depressive disease, is a mental health condition characterized by significant mood swings from mania (or hypomania) to depression (or vice versa). It affects about 1-2% of the population and can have a substantial influence on a person's everyday life, relationships, and capacity to function. Identifying bipolar disorder triggers and early warning signals is critical for properly managing the condition and preventing episodes from becoming severe.

Triggers are events, settings, or conditions that can induce a bipolar disorder patient to have a mood episode. Stress, lack of sleep, changes in habits, medication changes, substance addiction, and interpersonal conflict are all common factors. Understanding your personal triggers and understanding how to manage them might help you avoid mood swings and keep your symptoms under control.

Subtle changes in mood, behavior, or physical symptoms that may suggest the onset of a mood episode are known as early warning signs. Recognizing these warning signs early can help you take action to avoid a full-blown episode. Early warning indicators differ from person to person, but some frequent ones are:

- **Sleep pattern changes:**People with bipolar disorder may suffer sleep pattern variations, such as sleeping less or more than normal.

- Increased energy or restlessness: People with bipolar disorder may feel overly energetic or restless during a manic or hypomanic episode.

- **Significant changes in appetite or weight:**Significant changes in appetite or weight can indicate a mood episode.

- **Difficulty concentrating or making decisions:**During a mood episode, people with bipolar disorder may have difficulty concentrating or making decisions.

- **Withdrawal from social activities:**During a mood episode, people with bipolar disorder may avoid social events or become isolated.

- **Mood swings:**Bipolar disorder can be characterized by rapid fluctuations in mood, such as feeling incredibly pleased one moment and then becoming unhappy or irritated the next.

- **Suicide thoughts or behavior:**During a depressed episode, people with bipolar disorder may have suicidal thoughts or engage in self-harm.

If you or someone you know is suffering from any of these symptoms, it is critical that you seek professional care. Early intervention can help prevent episodes from becoming severe and improve persons with bipolar disorder's long-term outlook.

Chapter 7 Managing Depression

Understanding depressive episodes

Individuals with Bipolar Disorder may experience melancholy, hopelessness, worthlessness, and exhaustion during a depressive episode. Understanding Bipolar Disorder's depressive periods is critical for controlling the condition and enhancing the quality of life.

Depressive episodes in Bipolar Disorder can be devastating and linger for several weeks or months. They may cause individuals to lose interest in previously enjoyed activities, to have problems sleeping or to sleep excessively, to suffer changes in appetite, and to have difficulties focusing. Depressive episodes can lead to suicidal ideation in severe circumstances.

It is critical to recognize that depressive episodes in Bipolar Disorder differ from those in Major Depressive Disorder. While the symptoms may be similar, those suffering from Bipolar Disorder also have manic or hypomanic episodes, which are periods of heightened or irritated mood. These events must be considered while diagnosing and treating Bipolar Disorder's depression periods.

Depressive episodes in Bipolar Disorder are often treated with medication, such as mood stabilizers and antidepressants, as well as psychotherapy, such as cognitive-behavioral therapy. Working closely with a healthcare professional to discover the correct treatment plan for the individual is critical, as treatment can differ depending on the type and degree of symptoms.

Changes in lifestyle may also help with depressive episodes in Bipolar Disorder. Regular exercise, a healthy diet, and enough sleep can all help improve mood and alleviate symptoms. It is also critical to avoid drugs and alcohol, which can exacerbate symptoms and interfere with medicine.

In conclusion, recognizing depressive episodes in Bipolar Disorder is critical for controlling the disorder and enhancing the quality of life. Medication and psychotherapy are commonly used in treatment, but lifestyle changes can also be beneficial. Collaboration with a healthcare practitioner is vital for determining the best treatment plan for the individual.

Coping strategies for managing depression

Depression may be a crippling disorder that interferes with many parts of a person's life. It can make daily activities difficult, have an influence on relationships, and have a negative impact on one's overall quality of life. Coping strategies for depression can help people manage their symptoms and enhance their overall well-being.

- **Seek Professional Treatment:**Seeking professional treatment is the first step in dealing with depression. This may entail seeing a therapist or psychiatrist who can advise on treatment choices such as medication and talk therapy.

- **Create a Support System:**Having a support system can be quite beneficial in dealing with depression. This could be family, friends, or a support group. Having friends to talk to and lean on through difficult times can bring comfort and lessen feelings of isolation.

- **Physical Activity:**Physical activity has been demonstrated to increase mood and alleviate depression symptoms. Physical activity, whether through regular exercise, sports, or yoga, can help people feel more energized and reduce stress.

- **Mindfulness:**Mindfulness practices, such as meditation, can assist to alleviate stress and improve sensations of relaxation. Mindfulness practices can also help people become more aware of their thoughts and feelings, which can aid in the identification and correction of negative thought patterns.

- **Get Enough Sleep:**Sleep is critical for general health and can have a big impact on mood. Individuals suffering from depression should strive for seven to nine hours of sleep per night. Developing a consistent sleep regimen and avoiding stimulating activities before bed can aid in the promotion of peaceful sleep.

- **Engage in Enjoyable Activities:**Depression can make it harder to find pleasure in formerly enjoyable activities. Activities that bring delight, such as hobbies or spending time with loved ones, can assist to improve mood and minimize depression symptoms.

- **Manage Stress:**Stress can aggravate depressive symptoms. Individuals who learn stress management strategies such as deep breathing or progressive muscle relaxation can better cope with challenges in their lives.

In conclusion, dealing with depression takes a multifaceted approach that includes obtaining professional treatment, building a support network, engaging in physical activity, practicing mindfulness, getting enough sleep, engaging in enjoyable activities, and controlling stress. These coping skills can assist people in managing their symptoms and improving their general well-being.

Chapter 8 Coping with Anxiety and Panic Attacks

How are anxiety and panic episodes linked to Bipolar Disorder?

Individuals with Bipolar Disorder, a mental health disorder characterized by significant mood fluctuations ranging from manic or hypomanic periods to depressed episodes, are prone to anxiety and panic attacks. In fact, evidence reveals that up to 50% of people with Bipolar Disorder also have considerable anxiety symptoms.

Anxiety is defined by feelings of fear, anxiety, and apprehension, whereas panic episodes are characterized by abrupt and acute fear or discomfort that can continue for many minutes. Physical signs of panic attacks include a racing heart, sweating, shaking, and shortness of breath.

Anxiety and panic attacks are linked to Bipolar Disorder in one way: they are associated with the disorder's manic or hypomanic episodes. Individuals may have rapid racing thoughts, elevated activity levels, and grandiose notions during manic or hypomanic episodes, which can cause feelings of fear or panic.

Furthermore, evidence suggests that people with Bipolar Disorder who have anxiety or panic attacks are more likely to have more severe and frequent episodes of mania or depression.

During the depressive phase of Bipolar Disorder, anxiety, and panic attacks can occur. Individuals may suffer feelings of grief, helplessness, and worthlessness during this period, which can lead to feelings of anxiety or panic.

Anxiety and panic disorders are also possible co-occurring disorders with Bipolar Disorder. Individuals may feel anxiety or panic symptoms outside of their manic or depressive periods in certain circumstances, making it difficult to manage the symptoms of both diseases concurrently.

Anxiety and panic attacks in people with Bipolar Disorder are often treated with a mix of medication and treatment. To alleviate anxiety or panic symptoms, medications such as benzodiazepines or antidepressants may be used, while therapy such as Cognitive Behavioural Therapy (CBT) can help individuals develop coping mechanisms and manage their symptoms more effectively.

In conclusion, anxiety and panic attacks are prevalent in people with Bipolar Disorder and can be caused by the disorder's manic, hypomanic, or depressive phases. A combination of medication and counseling is usually used to treat both the symptoms of Bipolar Disorder and the related anxiety or panic attacks.

Coping mechanisms for anxiety and panic attacks

People suffering from bipolar disorder may also have anxiety and panic attacks, which can exacerbate their condition. Coping methods for anxiety and panic episodes during bipolar disorder can aid in symptom management and overall quality of life.

Here are some coping strategies for those with bipolar disorder who are experiencing anxiety or panic attacks:

Relaxation and mindfulness practices: Relaxation and mindfulness techniques can assist reduce anxiety and stress. Deep breathing exercises, meditation, progressive muscular relaxation, and guided imagery are examples of these techniques.

- **Regular exercise:**Regular exercise is a powerful technique for treating anxiety and depression, which are common in bipolar disorder. Exercise can assist to reduce stress, boost mood, and encourage better sleep.

- **Cognitive-behavioral therapy:**CBT can assist individuals in identifying and changing negative thought patterns and behaviors that contribute to anxiety and panic episodes. CBT can also help people develop coping strategies to deal with anxiety and panic episodes when they happen.

- **Medication:**A healthcare provider may prescribe medications such as benzodiazepines, antidepressants, and antipsychotics to assist treat anxiety and panic attacks. Working together with a healthcare provider to determine the best appropriate medication and dose for individual needs is critical.

- **Supportive relationships:**Individuals suffering from bipolar disorder can benefit from supportive interactions with family, friends, and mental health specialists. Listening, delivering practical assistance, and providing emotional support are all forms of support.

- **Self-care:**Self-care can assist people with bipolar disorder manage their symptoms and enhancing their overall health. Getting enough sleep, eating a good diet, avoiding drugs and alcohol, and indulging in hobbies that offer joy and fulfillment are all examples of self-care activities.

Finally, coping methods for anxiety and panic attacks during bipolar disorder can help people control their symptoms and live better life. Working collaboratively with a healthcare practitioner to build a personalized treatment plan that fits individual requirements and preferences is critical.

Chapter 9 Relationships and Bipolar Disorder

Communicating with loved ones about Bipolar Disorder:

Communicating with loved ones about one's bipolar disorder can be difficult, but it is essential for effectively managing the disorder and sustaining healthy relationships. This post will go through several methods for discussing bipolar disorder with loved ones.

- **Inform your family and friends about bipolar disorder:**One of the most important things you can do to properly communicate about bipolar disorder with your loved ones is to educate them about the condition. Share information on bipolar disorder symptoms, treatment choices, and how it might affect your life. This will assist your loved ones in better understanding your condition and providing necessary support.

- **Be frank and truthful:**It might be tough to discuss your experiences with bipolar disorder with your loved ones, but being open and honest with them is vital for creating trust and understanding. Openly and honestly express your thoughts and feelings, and be willing to listen to your loved ones' concerns and questions.

- **Set firm boundaries:**Living with bipolar disease can be difficult, and it's critical to set clear boundaries with your loved ones. Inform them of what you require and when you require it, as well as your constraints. This will assist your loved ones in knowing your requirements and avoiding misunderstandings.

- **Make use of "I" expressions:**Try to utilize "I" statements rather than "you" comments when expressing your experiences with bipolar disorder. For instance, rather than expressing, "You don't understand what I'm going through," say, "I feel like I'm struggling to explain what I'm going through." This will allow your loved ones to grasp your point of view without becoming defensive.

- **Seek expert assistance:**Finally, in order to effectively manage your bipolar condition, you must seek expert help. Working with a therapist, taking medication, and joining support groups are all options. Involving your loved ones in your treatment plan can assist them in better understanding your illness and providing appropriate support.

To summarise, communicating with loved ones about bipolar disorder can be difficult, but it is critical for properly treating the condition and sustaining healthy relationships. You can establish a supportive and understanding atmosphere for yourself and your loved ones by educating them, being upfront and honest, creating clear boundaries, using "I" statements, and obtaining professional treatment.

Developing healthy relationships

Extreme mood fluctuations can result from the disease, making it difficult for persons with bipolar disorder to connect with others and form meaningful relationships. People with bipolar disease can, nevertheless, develop good relationships by taking certain steps and obtaining professional support when necessary.

Here are some pointers for bipolar illness patients on how to form healthy relationships:

- **Educate yourself:**If you have bipolar disorder, you should learn about the disorder and how it affects your relationships. Understanding your triggers, symptoms, and treatment options can help you communicate with people more effectively and make more educated relationship decisions.

- **Communicate openly:**Open and honest communication is essential for the development of healthy relationships. It is critical to express your sentiments and needs to your spouse or pals, as well as actively listen to their concerns and requirements. Communication can aid in the prevention of misconceptions and the development of trust.

- **Manage stress:**Stress can induce bipolar episodes and make maintaining healthy relationships difficult. It is critical to acquire effective stress-management strategies, such as mindfulness, exercise, and self-care activities.

- **Maintain a treatment plan:**Bipolar disorder necessitates continuing treatment, which may include medication, therapy, and lifestyle changes. It's critical to follow to your treatment plan and share any concerns or side effects with your doctor. A steady mood can assist you in maintaining healthy relationships and lowering your chances of mood fluctuations.

- **Build a support network:**Creating a support network of family, friends, and healthcare providers is an important part of developing good relationships. Having people around you who understand and support you might help you manage your health and stay positive.

- **Setting limits:**Essential for maintaining successful relationships. It is acceptable to decline invitations to social events or activities that cause your symptoms or make you feel uneasy. Setting boundaries can assist you in prioritizing your mental health while also maintaining healthy relationships.

- **Seek professional assistance:**If you are having difficulty developing healthy connections, it may be beneficial to seek professional assistance. A therapist or counselor can assist you in resolving relationship concerns as well as developing healthy communication and coping skills.

In conclusion, developing good relationships for people with bipolar disease necessitates a combination of self-care, communication, support, and professional assistance. It is possible to sustain meaningful connections and have a full life with the correct tactics and assistance.

Managing conflicts and stress within relationships

Bipolar disorder can be a difficult condition to handle, both for the individual suffering from it and their loved ones. Bipolar disorder can cause additional stress and tension in relationships. However, with the correct tools and tactics, it is feasible to handle relationship difficulties and stress throughout bipolar disorder.

To begin, it is critical to recognize that bipolar disorder can have unpredictable effects on a person's moods, energy levels, and behavior. This can impede communication and decision-making, leading to misunderstandings and disputes in relationships.

Communicating openly and honestly is one of the most crucial things you can do to handle disagreements and stress in relationships while suffering from bipolar disorder. This includes being willing to discuss your feelings and concerns in a calm and courteous manner, as well as being open to hearing your partner's point of view. Avoid blaming or criticizing each other and instead concentrate on finding solutions that work for both of you.

Another key method is to establish limits and routines that might aid in the management of bipolar disorder symptoms. Setting aside time for self-care, such as exercise or meditation, as well as ensuring adequate sleep and a good diet, may be included. Setting clear expectations about obligations and roles within the partnership may also be necessary so that everyone knows what is expected of them.

It is also critical to seek professional assistance when necessary. Working with a therapist or psychiatrist to design a treatment plan that can help control the symptoms of bipolar disorder is one option. It may also entail seeking couples or family counseling to improve communication and address any relationship difficulties that may be causing stress or conflict.

Finally, it is critical to practice self-compassion and patience with both yourself and your partner. Bipolar disorder can be difficult to manage, and it's crucial to understand that there will be ups and downs along the way. You may manage disagreements and stress within relationships with bipolar disorder and build a solid and supportive relationship by being kind to yourself and your partner and working together to discover solutions that work for both of you.

Chapter 10 Stigma and Advocacy

Addressing stigma and discrimination surrounding Bipolar Disorder

Extreme changes in mood, energy, and activity levels characterize it, and can cause severe disturbances in a person's everyday life. Unfortunately, persons with bipolar disorder frequently encounter stigma and discrimination as a result of misconceptions about the condition. This stigma can have a negative influence on their quality of life, making it more difficult for them to seek help and leading to feelings of isolation and humiliation. In this post, we will look at techniques to combat the stigma and discrimination associated with bipolar disease.

Education is one of the most effective strategies to combat the stigma and discrimination associated with bipolar disease. Many people are unclear of what bipolar illness is, how it affects people, and how to support people who have the condition. Education on bipolar disease can help dispel myths and stereotypes, leading to better empathy and understanding. This training can take place in a range of locations, including schools, businesses, and healthcare facilities. It can involve healthcare professional training programs, public awareness initiatives, and community outreach programs.

A personal narrative is another technique to combat the stigma and discrimination associated with bipolar disease. When people with bipolar disorder share their stories, it helps others understand the difficulties they endure and how the disorder affects their lives. By putting a human face on the condition and encouraging empathy and understanding, can help minimize stigma and discrimination.

Mental health advocacy groups can also play an important role in eliminating the stigma and discrimination associated with bipolar disorder. These organizations can advocate for public policies that benefit people with bipolar disorder, such as increased financing for mental health services, improved access to care, and anti-discrimination protection. They can also give persons with bipolar disorder resources and assistance, such as support groups, counseling services, and instructional materials.

Finally, the language and terminology used to characterize bipolar disorder must be addressed. Some phrases, such as "crazy" or "insane," can be harmful and stigmatizing. Instead, it is critical to employ honest, non-judgmental terminology that represents the condition's complexities. Encouraging a more comprehensive knowledge of bipolar disease can help eliminate stigma and discrimination.

To summarise, tackling the stigma and discrimination associated with bipolar disease necessitates a multimodal approach that involves education, personal storytelling, mental health advocacy, and careful wording. We can create a more inclusive culture that supports people with bipolar disorder and other mental health issues by working together to foster better understanding and empathy.

Advocating for yourself and others with Bipolar Disorder

Advocating for yourself and others with Bipolar Disorder is critical to ensuring that people with this condition receive the necessary support and care.

Here are some suggestions for advocating for yourself and others suffering from Bipolar Disorder:

- **Educate yourself on the condition:**It is critical to educate yourself about the symptoms, treatment choices, and resources available for Bipolar Disorder. Understanding the illness will allow you to communicate it to others, make educated treatment decisions, and advocate for yourself or others.

- **Seek expert help:**If you or someone you know is suffering from Bipolar Disorder, it is critical that you seek professional assistance. A mental health specialist can give an accurate diagnosis and provide an individualized treatment plan to help you manage your illness.

- **Be vocal about your needs:**It is critical to be vocal about your requirements, whether with your healthcare provider, job, or friends and family. Speak up about what kind of help you need to manage the disease, and don't be hesitant to ask for it.

- **Join a support group:**Individuals with Bipolar Disorder may benefit from joining a support group. It can create a secure environment for you to connect with individuals who understand what you're going through and can provide you with support and assistance.

- **Advocating for policies:** Support mental health, such as access to affordable mental health care and workplace accommodations, can help improve the lives of people with Bipolar Disorder and other mental health issues.

- **Combat stigma:**The stigma associated with mental illness can hinder people from seeking treatment and obtaining the necessary support. You may help lessen the shame and discrimination associated with Bipolar Disorder by speaking out against stigma and sharing your own experiences.

Finally, advocating for yourself and others with Bipolar Disorder is critical to ensuring that people with this condition receive the support and care they require. You may help persons with Bipolar Disorder by educating yourself, receiving professional care, being vocal about your needs, joining a support group, lobbying for policies that promote mental health, and combating stigma.

Chapter 11 Conclusion

Finally, "Above and Below the Extremes: Finding Stability with Bipolar Disorder" is an in-depth resource for those living with Bipolar Disorder, their loved ones, and mental health professionals. This book has offered a thorough overview of the various types of Bipolar Disorder, their symptoms, and their causes. It has also looked into several treatment approaches, such as medication management, psychotherapy, and lifestyle changes.

Practical coping tactics for episodes of hypomania, mania, and depression, as well as anxiety and panic attacks, are presented in the book. We've talked about how important it is to establish resilience and strong relationships, confront stigma and discrimination, and advocate for oneself and others.

While this book is not designed to replace medical advice or treatment, it is meant to encourage readers to take control of their recovery journey. We hope that the practical techniques and insights presented in this guide will assist readers in achieving stability, resilience, and full life beyond the highs and lows of Bipolar Disorder.

To attain mental well-being, we advise readers to continue seeking help, creating a strong support network, and practicing self-care. Remember that healing is a journey that must be approached with patience, perseverance, and compassion. We wish all readers the best in their quest for stability and a satisfying life with Bipolar Disorder.

www.ingramcontent.com/pod-product-compliance
Lightning Source LLC
LaVergne TN
LVHW021323200726
843509LV00002B/99